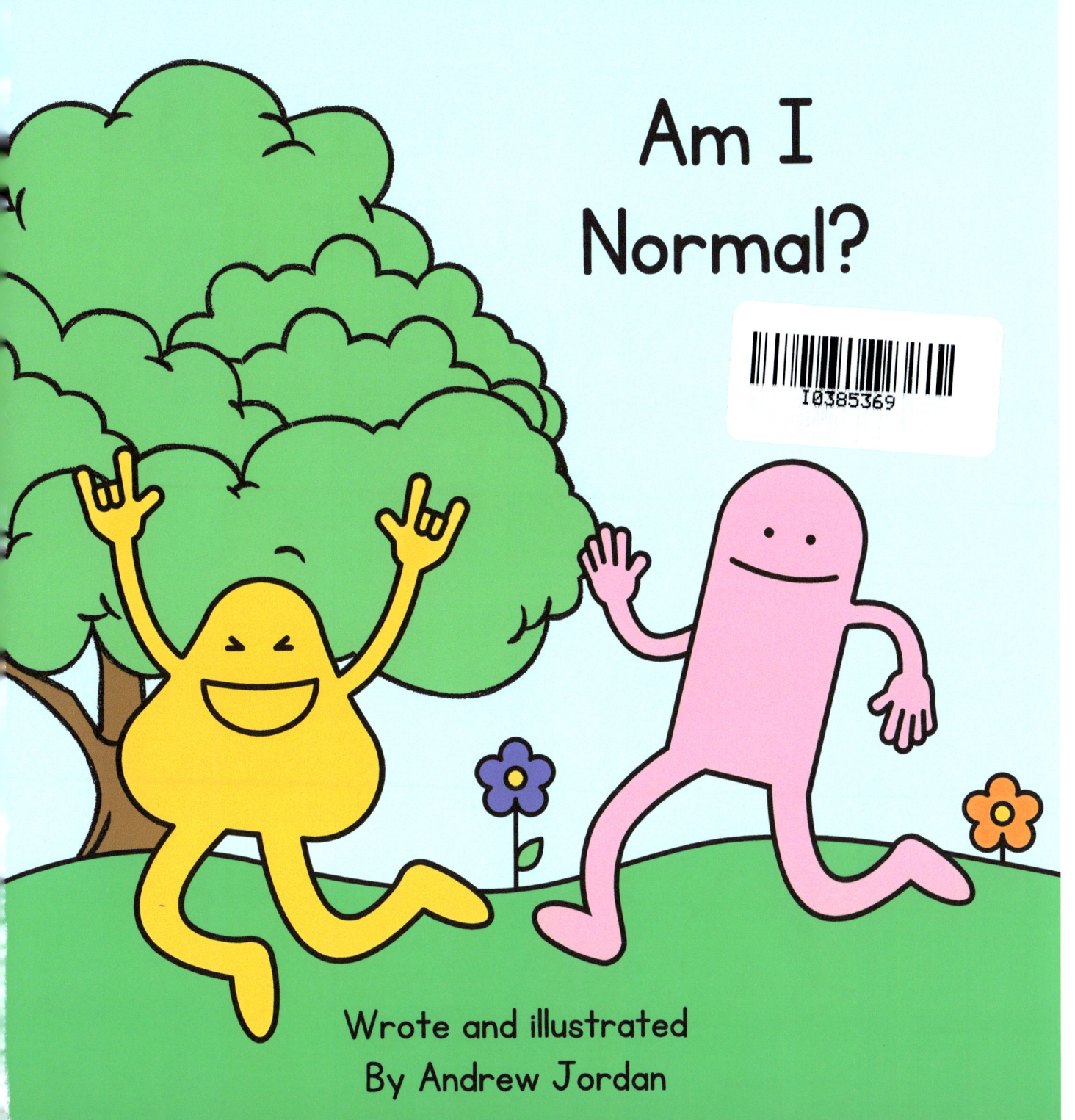

Bob met up with his friend John. Bob wanted to speak to John as he felt different, and he wanted to know if John felt the same.

Bob sees some of his friends. I will go and ask them.

Bob sees that they are all acting differently from each other.

Bob spoke to his friends.

Professor Paul was sitting, reading his favorite books.

Bob told Professor Paul, his questions surrounding being normal.

Bob asked the Professor, why he was not the same as his friends and why he didn't share the same interests or views too.

Professor Paul found these questions interesting.

Let's look on my computer.

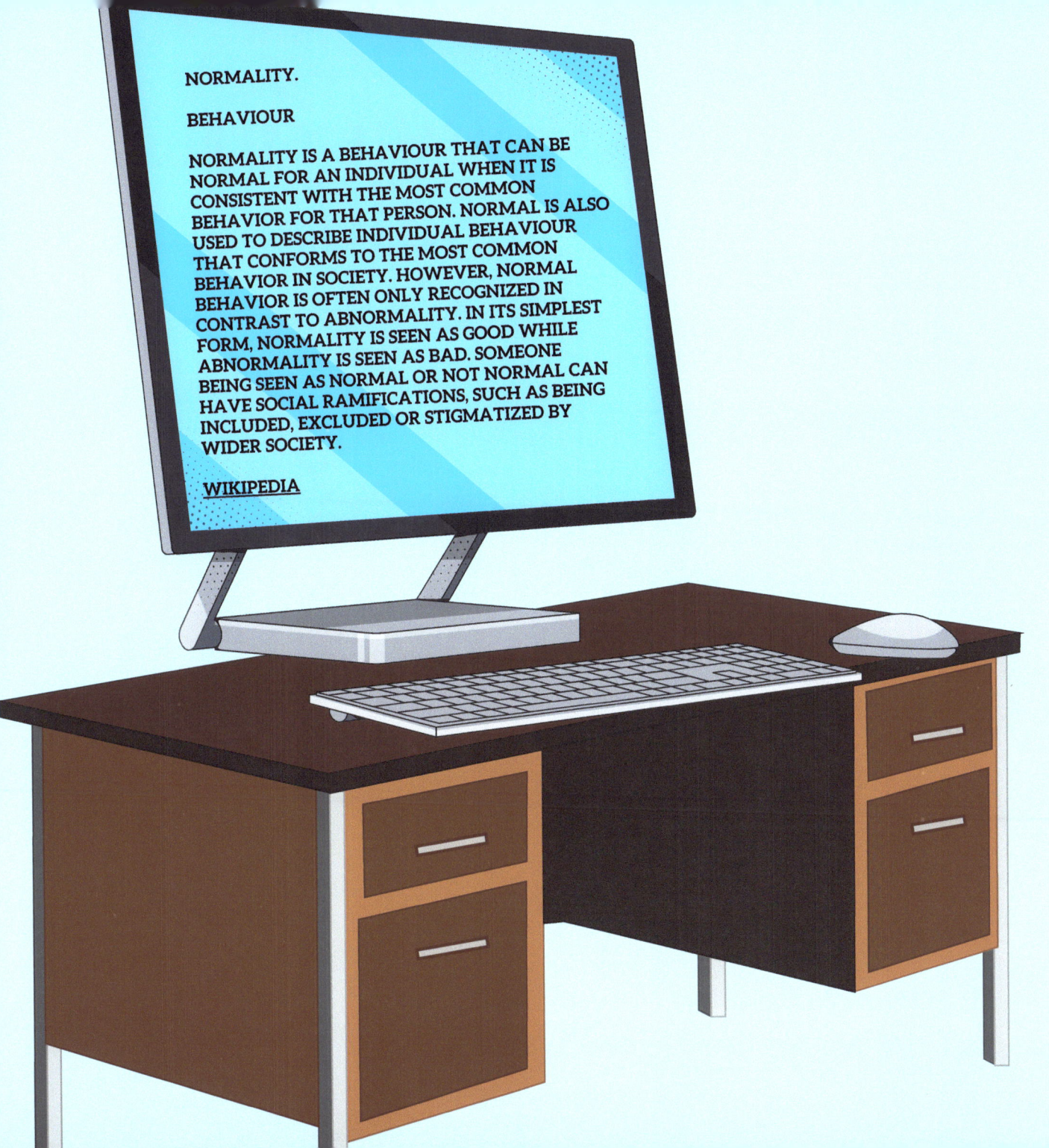

Let's see what others have said.

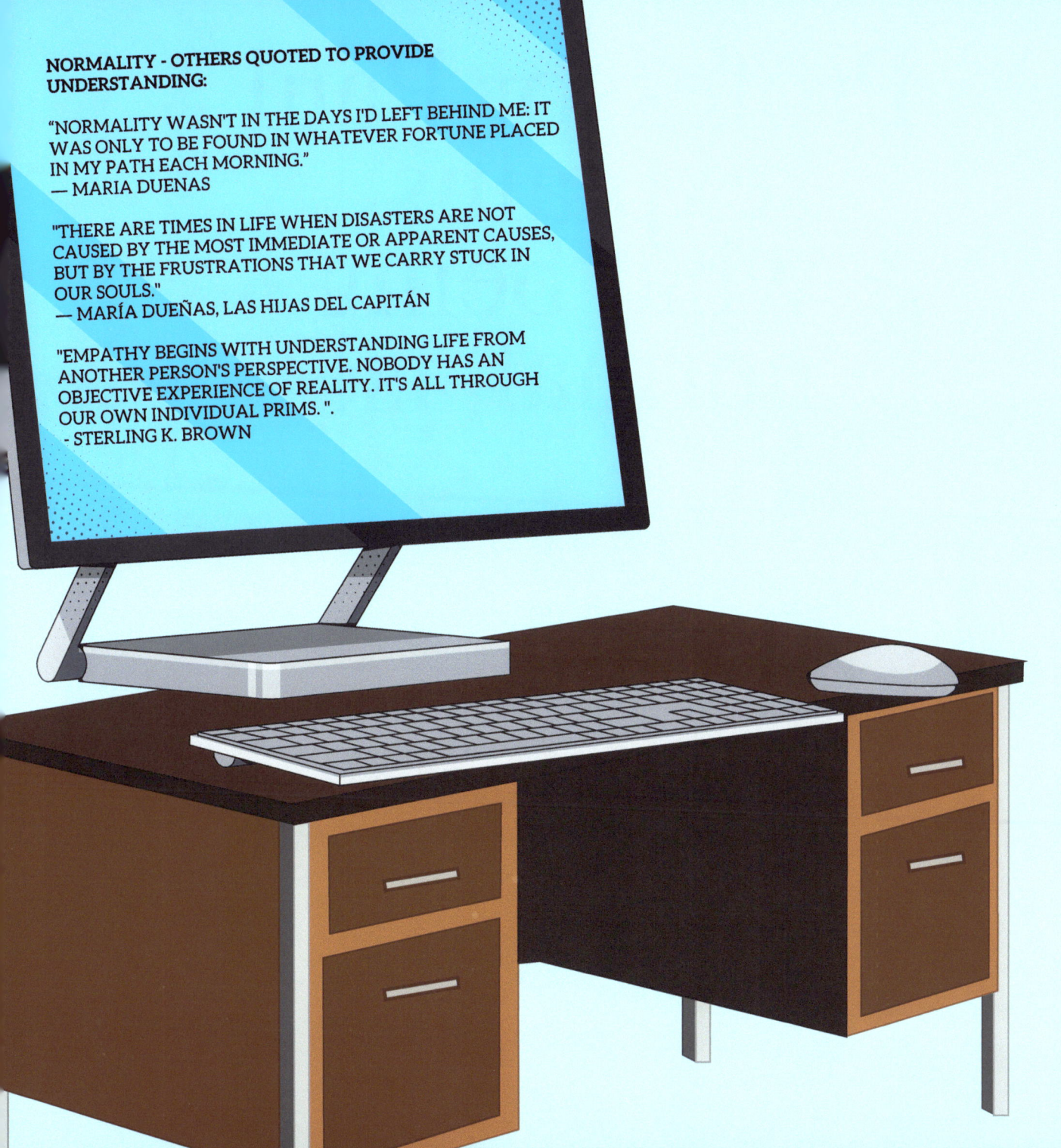

Professor Paul explains what being 'normal' is!

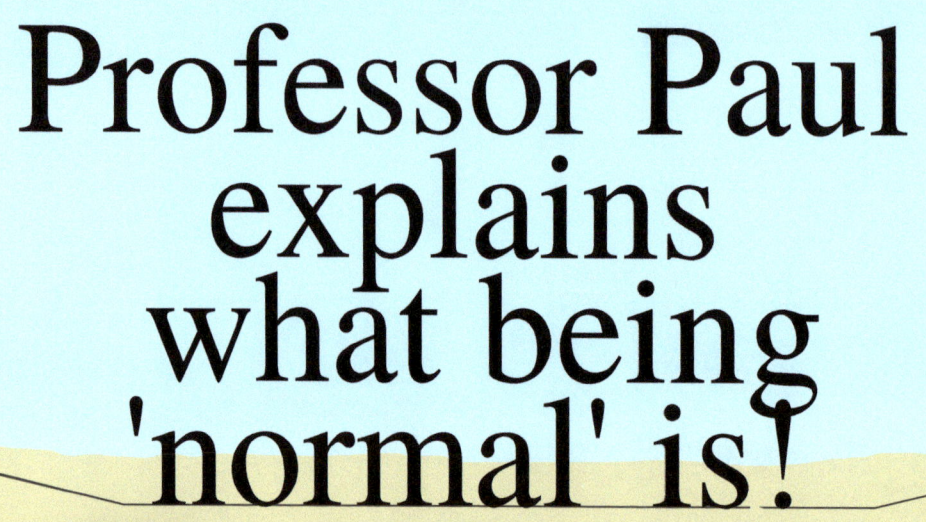

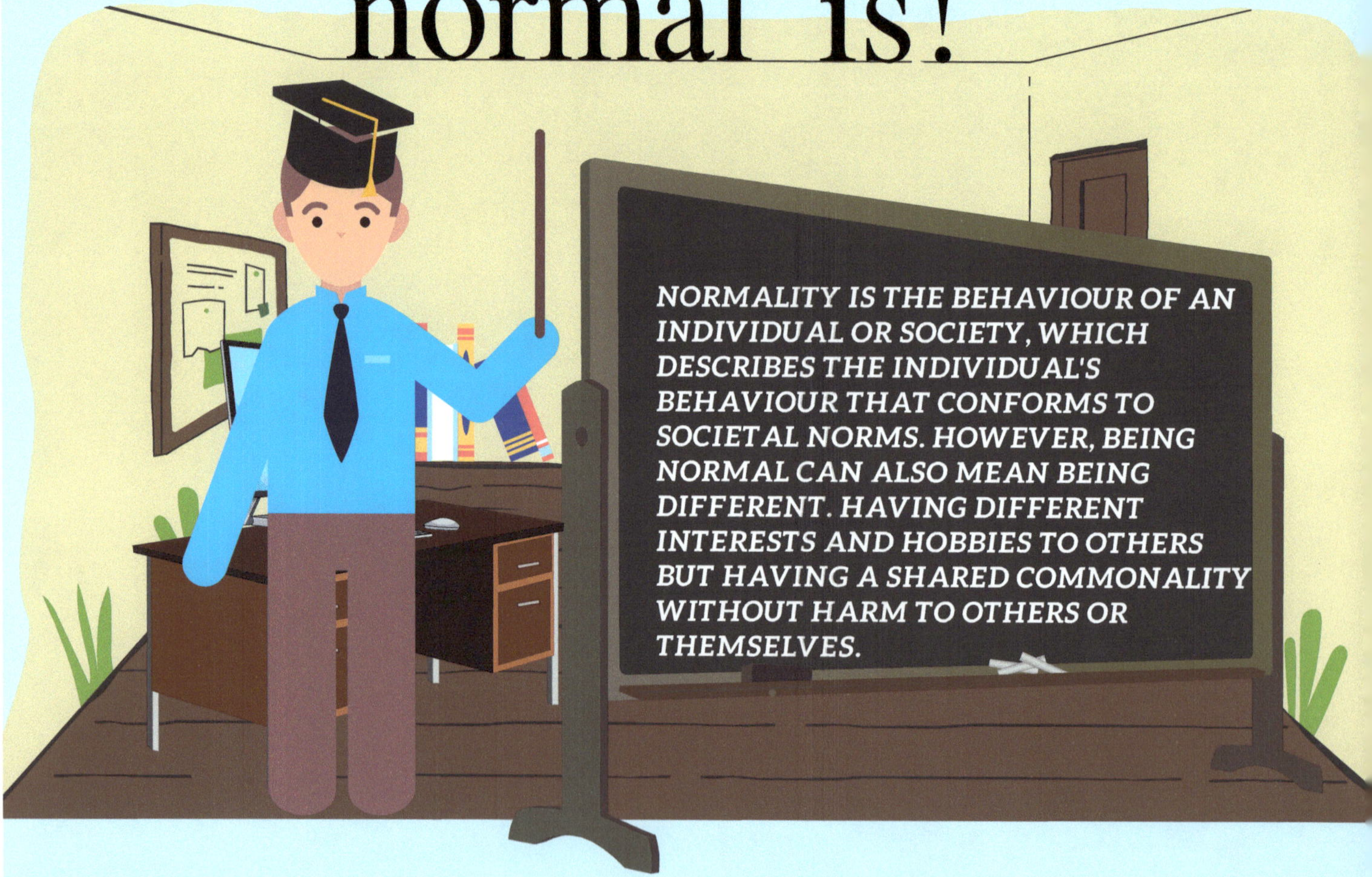

NORMALITY IS THE BEHAVIOUR OF AN INDIVIDUAL OR SOCIETY, WHICH DESCRIBES THE INDIVIDUAL'S BEHAVIOUR THAT CONFORMS TO SOCIETAL NORMS. HOWEVER, BEING NORMAL CAN ALSO MEAN BEING DIFFERENT. HAVING DIFFERENT INTERESTS AND HOBBIES TO OTHERS BUT HAVING A SHARED COMMONALITY WITHOUT HARM TO OTHERS OR THEMSELVES.

So, its okay to be different as long as it's accepted by society.

It's okay to have different views and hobbies as long as it doesn't hurt anyone.

REFERENCE : WIKIPEDIA CONTRIBUTORS. (2022, JANUARY 17). NORMALITY (BEHAVIOR). IN WIKIPEDIA, THE FREE ENCYCLOPEDIA. RETRIEVED 13:37, MARCH 15, 2022, FROM HTTPS://EN.WIKIPEDIA.ORG/W/INDEX.PHP?TITLE=NORMALITY_(BEHAVIOR)&OLDID=1066341041

MARÍA DUEÑAS (AUTHOR OF THE TIME IN BETWEEN). (N.D.). RETRIEVED NOVEMBER 1, 2022, FROM HTTPS://WWW.GOODREADS.COM/AUTHOR/SHOW/3295744.

PERSPECTIVE QUOTES - BRAINYQUOTE. (N.D.). RETRIEVED NOVEMBER 1, 2022, FROM HTTPS://WWW.BRAINYQUOTE.COM/TOPICS/PERSPECTIVE-QUOTES

www.ingramcontent.com/pod-product-compliance
Lightning Source LLC
Chambersburg PA
CBHW040022130526
44590CB00036B/60